Quick-as-a-V

New Testam...
Bible Stories to Color

stories by Andy Rector   **illustrated by Kathleen Patterson**

The Standard Publishing Company, Cincinnati, Ohio
A division of Standex International Corporation
© 1993 by The Standard Publishing Company
All rights reserved.
Printed in the United States of America

ISBN 0-7847-0122-9

MARY AND ELIZABETH

An angel told Mary, "You will have a baby boy. His name will be Jesus."

Mary went to see
her cousin Elizabeth.

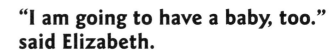

"I am going to have a baby, too."
said Elizabeth.
"His name will be John.
He will tell people about Jesus."

THE BIRTH OF JESUS
Joseph and Mary were tired. Where would they sleep?

"You may stay in my stable," said the innkeeper.

**Mary's baby, Jesus,
was born that night!**

FISHERMEN FRIENDS
Everyone wanted to be close to Jesus.

Jesus preached from a fishing boat.

Then Jesus helped
his friends catch fish.

THROUGH THE ROOF
Four men wanted Jesus to heal their friend.

They made a hole in the roof.

Jesus made the man well. Now he could walk!

THE GOOD SAMARITAN

Jesus told a story about a man who was robbed and hurt.

No one would stop to help the hurt man.

But one man did stop.
Jesus said that man was a good helper!